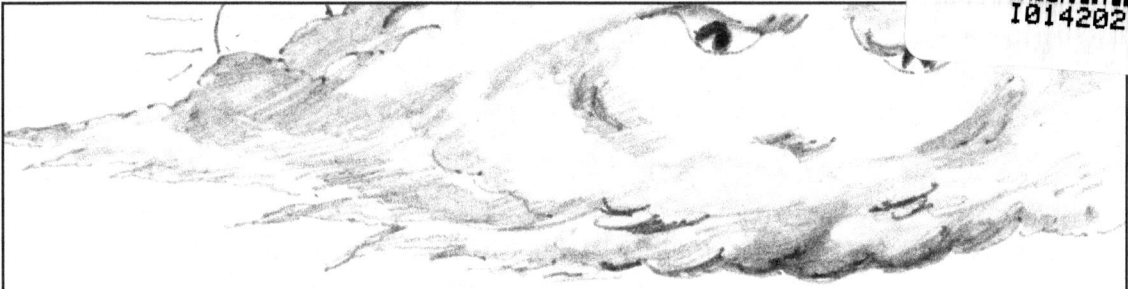

CAR-CAR'S JOURNEY

A Story for the Child in You

Bonita Y. McCall

ISBN: 978-1-935256-18-2

Published by BackDoor Books
PO Box 1652
Boone, NC 28607

Illustrated by William Moore

Graphic design by Abbie Frease
abbiefrease.com

For ordering directly from BackDoor Books contact us at ledgepress@gmail.com

For Clare and Evan

FOREWORD

There are many books that are "one-time reads." Some of them are books that you have to read in school. They are assigned to you. You must read them in order to pass the course.

Others are books you heard about, saw advertised or watched some celebrity rave about on television. You rush in excitement to get the book and then your excitement turns into disappointment when you discover that what you heard was hype. What you saw was "show" business—all appearance and no substance; and what was advertised was misleading.

Those books are books you only read one time. They are classified in your mental catalogue as "one-time reads."

There are other books, however, that are intriguing reads! *Car-Car's Journey* is an intriguing read. It is intriguing for many reasons.

First, it is intriguing because it packs such a tremendous wallop. It packs an enormous amount of truth into just a few short pages.

It packs plenty of meanings into incredibly short chapters. It packs philosophical gems onto page after page; and it packs such a profound literary punch that it leaves the readers instantly stunned and simultaneously drawn back to its pages (almost hypnotically) for more. *Car-Car's Journey* is a book that cries out to be read over-and-over again.

Car-Car's Journey is intriguing secondly because each time you read it you come away with different meanings, different insights and different glimpses of the author's artistic genius. Each time you read it, you see something that you had not seen before.

Each time you read it, you learn something new about your own life that you had not taken the time to learn before. Each time you read it, a different light bulb comes on deep in the recesses of your soul.

It is precisely this effect that Bonita McCall has attempted to evoke within the hearts and minds of the readers. She has done a masterful job and she has accomplished what she set out to do.

Car-Car's Journey is intriguing ultimately because it defies literary classification! Is it a children's book? Yes and no. Children can grasp its truths, but countless adults will be gripped by its penetrating insights.

Is it a religious book? Yes and no. Its spiritual truths are timeless and profound; but it can be read and appreciated by people of all faiths. (Jewish, Christian, Muslim, Buddhist, Hindu, Sikh, as well as practitioners of Candomblé, Vodun, Santeria, Yoruba and African-traditional religions.)

Its spiritual truths can not only be read and appreciated by people of all faiths, but can also be read, accepted and appreciated without debate by people of no faith!

This also is a goal that the author set-out to achieve. Bonita McCall is a woman of faith who is non-sectarian. She believes that divine truth can be found across denominational lines, nationalities, ethnicities, countries and cultures. She has proven her point powerfully in writing this poignant piece.

Car-Car's Journey strikes a nerve at the core of the reader's being and like the mysterious sirens of Jason and the Argonauts, its meanings keep calling the reader back for another visit to discover yet another nuance…and to be blessed by a book that has somehow become a "friend for life!"

This book is not a "one-time read." This book is more than a "must-read." This book is a companion that will engage you in endless conversations with your soul—with each conversation helping you to see beauty in this life while giving you glimpses of life that is eternal.

Rev. Jeremiah A. Wright, Jr.

Reverend Dr. Jeremiah A. Wright, Jr.
Pastor Emeritus, Trinity United Church of Christ
Chicago, Illinois

ACKNOWLEDGEMENTS

First of all I give honor to God and humble thanksgiving for my good fortune to have been born in an extraordinary family. From my grandmother, Grace B. Scott, to my parents, and my siblings, I have known (and been taught) unconditional love, the power of good humor, support in all my youthful (and not so youthful) endeavors, a love of Jesus, and a keen appreciation for the arts.

The fact that all my immediate family have left this earthly plane would be a devastating burden to bear were it not for the strength of their love, incredible wisdom, and the depth of their spirits infused with my own.

Without the love, support, and inspiration of Clarice Bernatsky, Jeanetta Swinney, William Moore, Anna J. Hicks, Schuyler Cunningham, Dyanne Elzia, Gloria K. Smart, Rev. Dr. J.A. Wright, Jr., and my son, Evan R. Edwards, *Car-Car* would have idled in neutral even longer than it did!

My heartfelt appreciation goes to publisher, Jeff Hendley and his son, "Bo," for believing in *Car-Car's Journey* and for making it possible to see it in print.

A very special "thank you" to Abbie Frease for her wonderful graphics creativity.

Bonita Y. McCall

AFFIRMATION
(Bonita's Vision)

Love is.
Truth prevails.
Justice is alive and moves beyond manipulation.
All wars—that kill—have lost their meaning and their thrust.
Their weapons become powerless; their weapons misfire and fail all direction.
Hate has lost its strength.
Its stranglehold on humanity becomes a weak and pitiful thing.
Violence has lost its strength too, and finds *no work available*.
Let all governments, everywhere, yield to the people
for the people's benefit first and foremost—
For what are governments, but people?!
Let the citizens be aware of their power and not misuse it.
The Earth is healing right now.
The awakened universal consciousness moves with us,
surrounding all naysayers, doubters, and other usurpers
in a circle of extreme light.
Their energies are quickly sent out of Earth to a safe harbor to be
nourished back to health
because
Love is!
Truth prevails.
Justice is alive and moves beyond manipulation!
Power to all people who practice being human.
They increase in love, compassion, super-consciousness, humor, purpose, powers of
forgiveness, humility, numbers, courage, vision, spirit, and heart.
They attain, retain, and sustain radiant health
and abundance according to God's riches in Glory
because Love reigns supreme.
God is Love.
Love is Life's Oldest Vibrating Energy!
And so it is this day on planet Earth,
located on a blue island
in the Cosmic Sea
of the Milky Way Galaxy.

CHAPTER I

The weather turned with a sudden treachery. The rain, which had started as an inconsistent drizzle, was turning into a freezing sleet. It slid down the windows of the sleek red sports car. Ice-laced drops kissed the car all over in soft, mushy splotches. The heavy rain defied the swishing dexterity of the little car's windshield wipers. Wet, slick curves in the road twisted and turned, giving The Driver all he could do to keep the car steady. Visibility dimmed with the fading sunlight as rolling clouds covered the last streaks of a bright morning, now fading to silvery gray and blue indigo.

The driver of the car was a very successful man. He had a big office in a very big building and he made many big decisions. He enjoyed the respect of those who worked for him, and he knew his worth. More than that, he was a good human being. He understood his life and he was not a greedy or selfish person. He had a wife who smiled at him, and a son who delighted him. It was his little son who christened the red sports car, "Car-Car."

The Driver had owned Car-Car a long time. He had been tempted by the newer, modern automobiles of today, but he couldn't quite convince himself to give up the pleasure and familiar enjoyment from being behind the wheel of his prized and rare little car. It had cost him lots of time and money over the years, but it ran with all its parts in humming harmony. The Driver drove it quite often though he could always choose to ride wherever he wanted to go in his big chauffeured sedan.

Car-Car enjoyed a good life because of the thoughtfulness and care it was given by The Driver. It was, therefore, a pleasure for Car-Car to give his owner good service in return. The years passed pleasantly, often with exciting trips and fun drives. One such trip found Car-Car in the hold of a great ocean liner. It was the only time Car-Car had been inside another vehicle, and on water instead of land, since his parts had been shipped to America. Car-Car was housed with several other shiny automobiles, below in the ship, and was visited by The Driver during the long voyage. The Driver would shine the little car with a soft cloth. He would check Car-Car's parts and clean them too. Car-Car relished the careful polishing and care from his owner. It made him beam, not only on the outside, but in all his well-kept parts. The Driver was glad to have the time to tinker with the machine that had become a reliable, smooth riding, great-looking, traveling companion. When he, and sometimes his wife, rode in Car-Car, they felt like they were riding in the groove of well-being and happiness.

Now, on this cold, wet stormy day just twenty miles from the clean, dry, warm garage Car-Car knew as home, the memories of sunshine and great voyages were all but forgotten.

The Driver had been encouraged by a sunny morning and had decided to drive Car-Car, just for pleasure, to the countryside near the big city where he worked and lived. The storm had begun furiously and without warning. The clouds had moved in wide fat herds, pushed swiftly across the sky by an errant and very wild wind. At first the sun seemed to be playing peek-a-boo with the darkening clouds, but it soon gave up the game and went to hide behind the growing gloom.

An alert and proven man behind the wheel, The Driver heeded the spontaneous mystery of weather and cutting his countryside visit short, he immediately headed back home. But the storm soon lost all ordinary intentions and quickly became a rare combination of weather-yowling phenomena! It seemed as though it could not make up its mind whether to snow or rain, be a tornado, a blizzard, or just split itself in two!

By the time The Driver thought to stop the car, pull off the road and wait out the storm, the pavement had become extremely icy. When another hairpin turn on the road curved into view, The Driver could not make Car-Car's tires follow his steering. Car-Car was not hugging the road, but was sliding! It was being whipped to the edge of the roadside with a fury! The little sports car and The Driver became one purpose. They tried to avoid going over in a deep ditch, but the effort was squashed by the icy falling snow—now turned to huge crystal flakes. Their patterns, so beautiful in prisms of crystallized realization, could not be appreciated by The Driver or Car-Car for they were like a power unto itself that took the full devastation and impact of the crash that followed.

Car-Car's indignant horn, a thin whine of its former self, woke The Driver to full awareness as lights and anxious voices reached his senses. Voices drifted through the shattered and splintered glass that once were Car-Car's windows. The Driver was grateful to wake to Car-Car's familiar horn and Car-Car felt his last gesture of giving reach its destination when The Driver woke up.

Before he ventured to move his wet, shocked body, The Driver listened to a soft hissing sound coming from Car-Car. It was getting slower and lower. It was a sad sound. The Driver gazed in disbelief as smoke rose from Car-Car's hood. He watched unhappily as plumes of smoky steam puffed, skittered and streamed in tired tendrils from his ruined, once beautiful, Car-Car.

A miracle! A miracle! An absolute miracle, said the people who saw the car and took The Driver to the hospital. The Driver had gotten out of the wreckage that once was his car, with only a scratch on one arm!

"A miracle!" said the doctor at the hospital where The Driver had been taken.

"A miracle!" said his smiling, loving wife.

"A miracle!" cried his delighted son.

"A miracle!" joined The Driver, and he was very happy to be alive.

CHAPTER II

Now the twisted, broken wreckage of the little sports car sat forlornly in a junk yard. Its' sad journey earlier, when it had hung unceremoniously from the rear end of a proud and powerful tow truck, was over.

"Well," sighed Car-Car, "I should not complain. I've had a grand and glorious life." He looked around at the other cars around him and he sighed again. "I really shouldn't complain. I'm much older than most all these other piles of sorrow and broken-down junk. If this is the way it ends, I'll just have to get used to it." And the little car sighed so deeply, its rear-view mirror, hanging on a thread of wire, clang-a-langed to the crunched-up dashboard.

"You certainly will have to get used to it!" came a gravel-sounding voice from across the litter strewn aisle. Car-Car was startled. He looked across the aisle and saw a dilapidated compact model, nearly a dozen years younger than Car-Car. The Compact went on, "We sit here, day and night, in all kinds of weather and we rust and rust. Sometimes one gets taken away and we make up stories about where that one has gone or what might be happening to it. Sometimes they take a bunch of us and throw us all together in a huge and terrible machine that crunches us up 'til we're just about that big!" For emphasis, The Compact spit a tiny screw toward Car-Car.

"Oh no!" cried Car-Car, "That sounds awful!"

"No matter," laughed The Compact, "I'm still free because I don't sit around looking sad and unhappy. You've got to look as useful as possible. Think useful! That's the way!"

Car-Car was dumbfounded. What did The Compact mean he was free!? Then Car-Car was astounded again because he realized he was actually talking to another car! In fact, he couldn't remember talking at all. And here he was having a conversation with, of all things, a happy piece of a junked vehicle in the most unlikely place possible! Not only that, Car-Car reckoned, The Compact had imagination! Car-Car reasoned it must be that because all the other wrecks were either laughing at The Compact or grumbling in an eerie chorus of rattles, dings, and dents! Car-Car had never had to use his own imagination because his life heretofore had been a dream.

The Compact stole glances of pure enjoyment at the unhappy, broken little red car. He knew that it had been a beauty before its accident. He had only seen one auto like Car-Car before and that was at an auto show where he himself had been on display, but he also knew—because he was wise and shrewd—that Car-Car was unaware of anything outside a very sheltered existence. The Compact, on the other hand, had been around a lot of blocks and race tracks in a lot of cities. He was an old pro and a one-time big winner.

He saw Car-Car beginning to go into rust-mode and rust-mode, to The Compact, was the worse thing for any car that found itself in a junk yard because it mildewed the spirit. The Compact liked the little red sports car and tried to give him courage. "And another thing," he said, as though there had not been a break in the conversation, "nobody knows what happens to the ones who get taken away from here by some human who comes browsing around. It could be something wonderful like being completely overhauled and on the road again…Vrooom-vroooom!" The Compact reveled in the moment's memory of revving up.

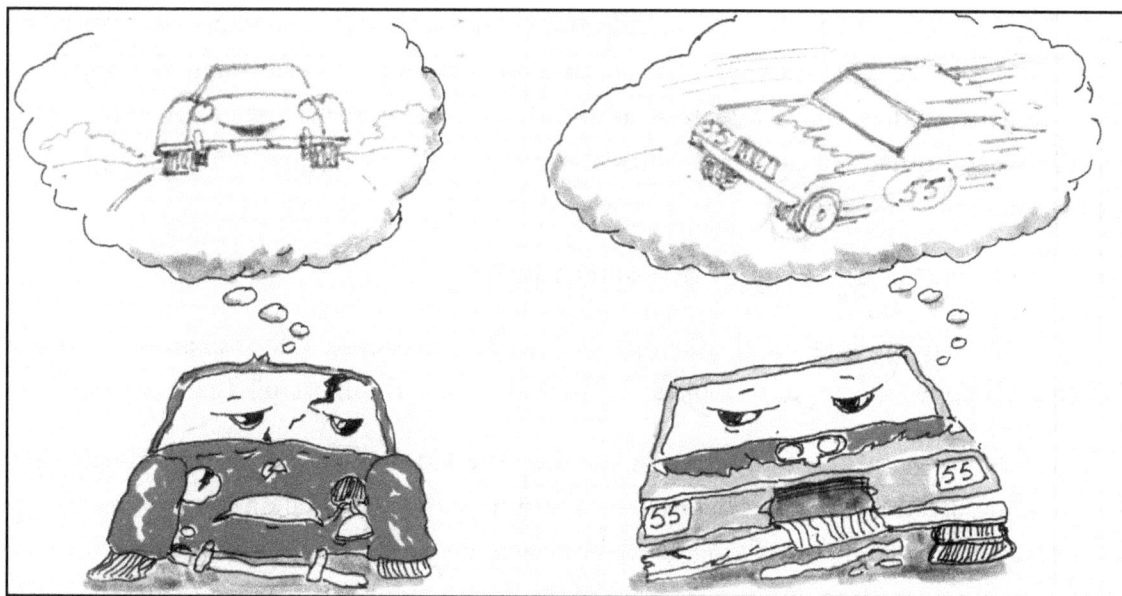

Car-Car almost got happy. Even in his present circumstances he could not help but feel the powerful enthusiasm of The Compact. Then he looked again at the pathetic mess of The Compact. Half its parts were missing. It had no wheels and rested like a flat, squat, dusty shell on the ground. It had one door that hung limp on broken hinges and the door window was half-way rolled up with only shreds of glass remaining. Its headlights were sunken, busted out sockets. Car-Car's own condition was just as pitiful and he began to sink into a terrible sadness. The Compact, however, was so cheerful Car-Car couldn't manage to remain sad very long.

As the days went by, Car-Car and The Compact observed many things. Most of the discarded, broken automobiles sat dejected during the day and grumbled through the night. Car-Car noticed that the huge and terrifying crane indiscriminately claimed parts of the rows of metal bodies and clamped their inert pieces in its huge jaws for one big swing around the junk yard, then down, SMASH, into the scary machine that squished everything into a wrinkled flatness.

"What's the sense in looking useful and proud when we've ended up in this place? No use fooling ourselves. It's the…," Car-Car began to stutter, "the…the old giant crusher for all of us!" And Car-Car could hardly hold back the tears that he knew would further his rust. But the strong enthusiasm of The Compact would not be dimmed. "Sometimes," he said, "someone will come here looking for not a whole car, but only a part of a car. Well, I say, put your whole self in whatever part that is. I mean, it is still YOU!"

The Compact was in a zone now and he continued in the face of Car-Car's awe. "You just might receive all new parts to go with the rest of you if you get taken away from this place. Put yourself in useful gear and think useful. That way, if someone takes a piece of you, you won't get lost. You'll be smaller, that's for sure, but you know, size is not what makes us who we are anyway! I'm still The Compact even though I don't have half the parts I was born with nor do I look that good, but I am still good, don't 'ya know." His voice got quiet and his speech slowed. Then he went on. "I talk more these days, but then that's the way it is now. I don't think we autos talk much until we stop being driven." He started into thinking about his instant philosophy and now became very still.

That night the junk yard was shrouded in a haze of lovely ground fog. It drifted and crept between the rows of wreckage. Car-Car thought the battered autos seemed to be floating among the clouds. He thought of The Driver and the clouds that had brought his downfall. He wondered how clouds could be so beautiful and carry such fury too. He was glad for his new friendship with The Compact. It kept him from focusing on the old giant crusher. He wanted to believe The Compact, but he could not imagine such a rescue.

The Compact told him to practice thinking "useful" and Car-Car tried.

Now in the midst of a growing mystery shrouded in a ground-foggy night, Car-Car did not want to disturb The Compact's reverie, but a nagging question haunted him.

"Compact," Car-Car began, "If we succeed at feeling useful but no one comes to take us away from here, we must face the old giant crusher. Isn't that right?"

The Compact answered a terse "yes." Car-Car went on, "Well since that is true, won't our efforts be in vain?"

The Compact seemed to rise up on his rusted wheel shafts. "Absolutely not," he answered. "Put your whole self in whatever parts that are being used and just go! That's the way to live! If life finds you in a flattened, pancake of a shape, you'll still be you—just shaped differently. Who knows what else you might become from that shape? Although I think it better to leave here with the future making you a new ride, I know this is not the end. Not even the old giant crusher can make such a thing true. That's why, even though we seem to just be sitting here, I make myself useful by encouraging myself—and others too—that we must have a purpose even if it is only to wait"

Car-Car thought The Compact must be very wise. He put new and old questions behind him for the moment and started concentrating on feeling useful.

CHAPTER III

The days were growing warmer and longer. Spring was in the air. Car-Car's only movement came from being inched closer to the old giant crusher or being dumped upon with other bits and pieces of wreckage. Still, Car-Car had a growing sense of usefulness and pride. The more he practiced, the more he felt intact, even though in all actuality he was falling apart. There were times when Car-Car allowed himself to grow lost in memories. He recalled the time The Driver had taken him on the ocean voyage where he lived three glorious weeks in the hold of a great ship. He remembered the lull of the waves and the colorful lure from cruising on scenic foreign roadways far, far from home.

He thought about the stories The Compact had shared of former days as a great stockcar racer and how his owner had "souped him up" with all the fastest and latest equipment of the day. He talked about incredible speeds and "winning races" with the same reminiscent glow that Car-Car felt when he thought about journeying across the sea. He wondered at The Compact's lively personality and determination in these circumstances when he had lived such an exciting and glorious past. Now facing an uncertain future Car-Car was amazed and impressed with The Compact's resolve.

The Compact told Car-Car that he was certain he had been constructed by "happy hands." Car-Car told him he was just as certain he couldn't recall being constructed at all, but he was also certain he would never forget his driver. Then The Compact told Car-Car something that Car-Car knew he would always treasure.

The Compact told Car-Car that this certainty of his, remembering his driver so fondly, should be used as the fuel that would energize his efforts to always think useful.

And so it was, on an early spring day that something extraordinary happened to Car-Car right in that piled up heap of a junk yard. Car-Car was sitting in the morning sun feeling more useful than he had in weeks. He had no idea that he was about to begin a whole new journey.

CHAPTER IV

The Artist was a sculptor and a painter. She had worked for several years as such and she was drawn to metal and wood. She saw art everywhere and in everything. She recognized art even in the litter strewn about in the city as well as along country lanes and the wind-swept beaches of the shore. She felt the energetic meeting of acetylene torch on twisted steel. She directed the tap-tap hammering of tools against an object's surface—now chisel, now sandpaper, now polish, now solder—as she arranged shape and mass. She ran skilled hands over surfaces, coaxing and bending form, renewing life from seeming inanimate things.

When The Artist stepped in front of Car-Car she knew instinctively that this was just the right object for her. It gave her the very correct feeling she was looking for. That same afternoon she returned with a truck and Car-Car, sans one wheel, four tires, a rear-view mirror, seats, and one door, said goodbye to The Compact.

The Compact saw that Car-Car was unsure and seemed reluctant to leave. He didn't want Car-Car's spirit to mildew from sadness and so he reminded his friend that he should not mourn this change. "You don't have all your parts, but this is okay. You will never need a rear-view mirror again because you are going to spend your new life looking ahead!"

"Think useful," urged The Compact. "Wherever you go, whatever you come to, always be as useful and as happy as you can be!" Car-Car knew that The Compact would remain a part of his best memories and his friend no matter what. It took all of his strength not to leave part of his true essence in the junk yard, locked in the broken pieces of his old self, but he knew that part of his heart would remain forever with his new friend.

Even though he had practiced hard at feeling useful while waiting, it was still difficult not to want all that was left of him to go with the rest of him in the truck with The Artist. Then he recalled something The Compact had told him over and over. It was only two days before that he had said it again: "It happens that friends can be separated by life changes, but the best part of friendship is that it lives forever in the friends. Friendship makes you stronger, able to face whatever life offers with confidence." Car-Car put his own two-and-two together right then. He figured that the reason friendship has a "ship" in it is to give the friends a way to sail away and back again on the currents and waves of life. Meeting a friend, for Car-Car, was a mighty good thing even if that meeting happened in a junk yard. Now Car-Car could relate the big ocean liner voyage and The Driver, to the "friendship" that would sail him away from the junk yard and The Compact.

Car-Car mustered up all of his courage, took heed of all he had learned and went totally into the waiting truck. The Artist sat beside the truck driver. She looked back at Car-Car and smiled. She already had an idea of it being turned into art. Car-Car looked at The Artist. He felt a new kind of comfort oozing from her to him and he felt something else new. He was hundreds of pounds lighter! He had lost a lot of weight, but he felt curiously strong.

As the truck rumbled along through the city, Car-Car thought of The Driver, The Compact, the junk yard, his old home in the big warm garage, and the lessons he had learned. Just like the storm that had changed his life, this new day had come unforeseen with all new changes. Things would never be the same, but in some ways things were better. He had made a friend, an accomplishment he thought better than being born a Bentley! He had been delivered to a junk yard hanging upside down on the back of a tow truck. Now he was rescued from the junk yard, and even though he was yet attached to a truck, he was now riding on the truck's long back bed with some semblance of dignity.

When the truck reached The Artist's house, Car-Car was unloaded in a big back yard on a brick patio next to a very tall and ancient tree. A huge truck tire was swinging from the tree's thick branches. The tree was just coming into bloom and Car-Car could see the blue sky through its budding, baby leaves. Four children ran from the house and curiously looked at the wreck of Car-Car, but they did not touch him. Their mother, The Artist, would leave him just as he was until she knew who he would become. Her children knew better than to rearrange their mother's works awaiting assignment.

The house and yard were in a kind of chaotic order. It was a modest house, nothing like the estate where he originally lived, but compared to the junk yard that had been his home for the past weeks, it was magnificent! He would have traded his left bumper to be able to tell The Compact of his good fortune, but then he realized that he no longer had a left bumper! In that moment Car-Car knew he had truly grown up because he really didn't mind not having his missing parts.

He liked the playful shrieks of the children and he was intrigued by the art works in the yard. Scattered here and there were sculpted pieces in wood and metal. Modern leaves of thin metallic sheets reached from their pedestals to the sky, semi-curled wooden poles intertwined with metal rings, old tables, works in progress like Car-Car, all inhabited the yard. In a corner nearest the house, a garage had been turned into The Artist's studio. Among and around all the various works of art, the children appeared and disappeared regularly amid laughter, tears, chatter and shared secrets.

The Artist studied Car-Car every day. She would walk around his parts, sometimes touching the trunk or running her fingers around the curvature of the dented hood. She would sit in front of Car-Car and close her eyes for long periods of time only to open them again, move her position to another angle, stare at Car-Car, and then close her eyes once more. Car-Car wondered what The Artist would do with him. He reasoned that if she had wanted to make use of him, he would look like an automobile again because that is how he saw himself. If that was so, then she should not have left so many of his parts in the junk yard. He felt like only a shell of his former self. Then he remembered his lesson and knew he was destined to resemble nothing familiar to a car. The shock of knowing this was in no way unpleasant, but even that surprised Car-Car. He was really beginning to understand that life is a continuous journey with all sorts of twists, turns, and circuitous routes.

As the weeks drifted by, Car-Car settled into a routine of trying to guess what The Artist had in mind for him. He looked at the other artworks and thought of his parts being bent into strange shapes. He found himself thinking of being overhauled, yet could not convince himself that this was a possibility. He certainly would never hold two humans in what was once his luxurious interior again, nor would he feel the smooth road spinning off his tires as in the days of old, but he still could not imagine himself as anything other than an automobile.

One day The Artist sat looking at Car-Car for a longer time than usual. She did not close her eyes, but she shook her head in a knowing way and she smiled and smiled. She wore coveralls and thick work gloves. The sun was a glowing half-circle of radiating orange beams on the horizon when The Artist suddenly pulled the remaining bumper—rusting dents and all—right off of Car-Car! She laid it down on the ground and began to carefully take other pieces off Car-Car. She laid each piece gently next to one another on the patio. For a moment Car-Car panicked. He didn't know which part of himself to put his essence in?! And then he knew that he could move from one piece to the other and that it was okay because The Artist would either use all the pieces or some of them. Either way, he knew he should remain calm and just leave the process and The Artist to creativity.

The Artist had been contemplating a new work, a large piece that would speak of the changes in the life cycle. It should be pure and simple, yet big and strong, and should suggest a well-used instrument or tool or conveyance. She silently pondered her idea as she gazed at Car-Car. He fit the bill in usefulness and size. The Artist knew the make of the car to be quite old and rare. Her intentions unfolded quietly until the plain sight of her creation was born in her imagination. Then she began to work.

The following day The Artist drew charcoal renderings of Car-Car on a large pad. She made notes next to the pictures as she walked back and forth and around Car-Car again and again. The next day The Artist made herself more familiar with Car-Car by touching all of its surfaces. She ran her hands over the parts of the car, and with her tools, began to disassemble Car-Car's parts while arranging the pieces here and there, or discarding little pieces altogether. Car-Car became so scattered he decided it was maybe a good time to sleep, perhaps to dream he was already whole again.

Then, on the fourth day, The Artist began to mold and remold the material stuff of the little car into a brand new idea. She already knew that as an artist, part of her own self would always be intermingled with the art she was creating; for in creating it, she was becoming somehow new too.

Soon the little car actually began to take a kind of shape. It went through fire and water and constant rubbing until it resembled anything but a car! Then it was partially painted in glistening coat after coat of shiny, enamel-like red paint, the same quality and color of its original paint job. Car-Car was thrilled and felt more whole and more useful than it ever had! He stretched his auto spirit in praise of usefulness whenever The Artist worked.

The Artist saved one crooked piece of Car-Car's body which she molded into a sort of circle. This piece she did not paint. It was about two feet in diameter and had formerly been part of Car-Car's hood. It had a misshapen hole in it. She sprayed several coats of heavy, clear gloss paint on the strange, dented piece with the rusting hole. The Artist riveted that piece to the top of the gleaming red marvel of sculpted art. It looked like an old, worn-out hat, half-cocked! It seemed out of place until it was gazed upon for a while. Then it came together like it was meant to be seen. The shiny sleek surfaces and the odd, dented "hat" balanced one another like a body in a new suit, traveling with all its old stuff packed precariously, but stately, on top of its head!

When it was all finished, The Artist had two assistants help her attach the new art of Car-Car to a huge white-painted, rough hewn block. On a small brass plate in the middle of the block were the words: Timeless Travel.

The years came and went as Car-Car basked among the works of art in the backyard of the modest house. The children grew and sometimes sat with friends under the tree or next to Car-Car on the patio.

Those years were not wasted on Car-Car. He did not have The Compact to talk with, but he had plenty of time to contemplate and assess his understanding of life. He came to recognize that everything served many different purposes during a lifetime. Nothing stayed one minute in the exact same way. Every moment was unique and timeless.

Though humanity had dominion over and mastered things, these same things had some control over humanity. It came to him that all things, both material and non-material, changed ever so subtly all the time, that matter only changed form but could not be totally obliterated. Even if annihilated by some manmade devastation or some earthly force, the very dust from any being wafted through the airwaves, coming to rest somewhere, temporarily part of something else. Everything that ever existed is still in residence—still at home, still a part of everything that is. Life was like a constant becoming! If he ever saw The Compact again, what a story he had to tell!

It was a good thing Car-Car had come to such a lofty understanding because he was about to be put to the test.

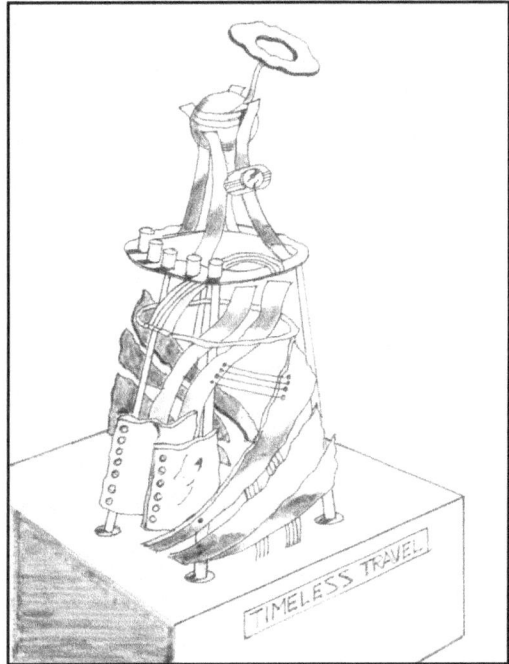

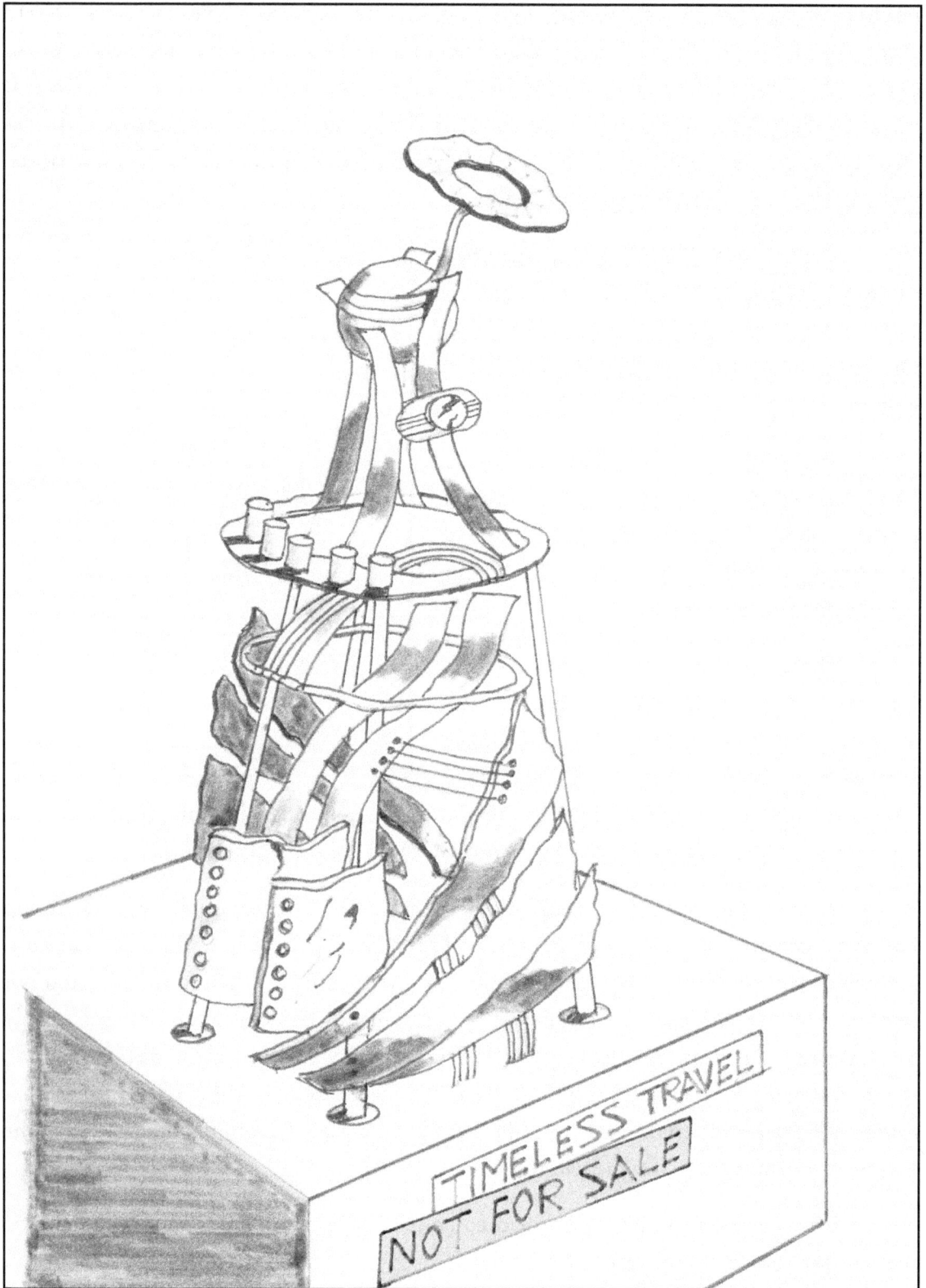

TIMELESS TRAVEL
NOT FOR SALE

CHAPTER V

The Artist went to PTA meetings, graduations, her children's special activities, and a day job while her children were in school. Besides these busy doings, she found time to work in her studio. She was very busy and only sold her art on occasion. Then one day she received a phone call from the gallery where she had two paintings and one of her sculpted works on view. A very famous collector had visited the gallery and liked her work. He wanted to see more of it. It was at long last the artistic break The Artist had been waiting for.

When The Collector came to the modest house to see The Artist's works, he had barely stepped from the back door when his eyes fell on Car-Car. He hardly noticed the other structures, but headed straight to Car-Car. There he stood for the longest time. The Artist had not intended to sell Car-Car. She was particularly fond of it. She found herself moving it further back, away from the patio, over the years. When buyers came to see her work she purposely put other things in the way of Car-Car so it would not be seen to good advantage. Somehow, however, potential buyers and admirers of art always singled it out so she put a "NOT FOR SALE" sign on it and put it back on the patio. The Collector had the eye of an eagle for the most appealing and outstanding works of art. When he saw Car-Car, he knew that it would be a much sought-

after piece of great value. When she saw his great interest in Car-Car, The Artist began her well-rehearsed spiel, but it didn't work. The Collector enticed The Artist with a price far more than she ever imagined. With four children on Earth and a husband in Heaven, the money offered by this collector would be a great boon. Not only that, but his name and reputation would further her sales and recognition as an artist to be taken seriously. It was too good an opportunity to walk away from, and so The Artist sold Car-Car to The Collector.

By this time one of the lessons that Car-Car knew for sure was to be true to himself. The fact was that he had no inclination to change any space he happened to be in that was pleasant—not if he could help it! Of course he also grew to know that he was not writing the script in which he was bound to play his part anyway, but that life itself was moving and changing, seemingly on its own mission—and taking him with it!

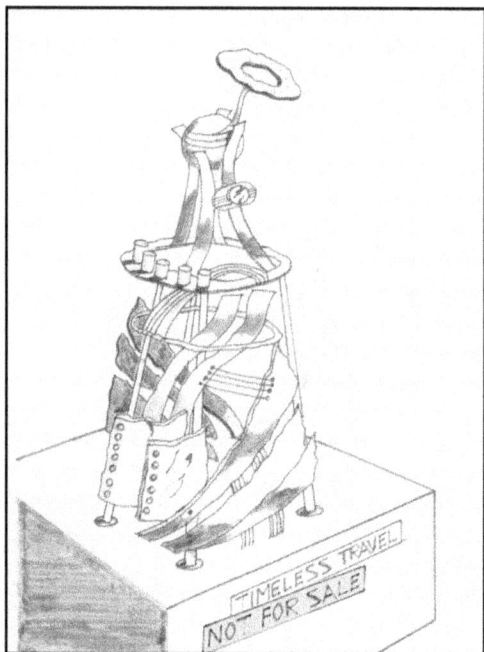

CHAPTER VI

The Collector owned many treasures. He had a mansion full of wonderful art. Car-Car found himself in a sunny atrium. His only companions were a large telescope standing on a platform next to glass doors that opened onto a balcony, a huge teakwood desk with a beautiful sailing vessel nestled inside a fat bottle on top of it, two big Egyptian-styled chairs, and one wall with a colossal painting of a great and furious sea rushing against towering cliffs.

Car-Car tried not to long for the backyard and the tree and the family. When night came and The Collector had wearied of gazing upon his new prize, Car-Car took to talking out loud just like that first night in the junk yard. Did birds come to visit the junk yard? No, they did not—that was in the backyard of The Artist's house. There were no birds in the garage of The Driver's estate and Car-Car didn't pay attention to birds on the road except when they pooped on his windshield! Wow, he thought, I used to have a windshield!? In the backyard of the modest house of The Artist, birds were like traveling musicians that came to perform their artistry regularly. It seemed somehow, that these natural warblers sang just for him. Some of the birds lived in the tree with the big truck tire hanging from it. Their songs and the melodies of their visiting kin never ceased to amuse and entertain Car-Car. He had not thought of the birds as unusual for a long time. Now suddenly in a new space, he thought his heart would break without birdsong nearby. "What is to become of me in this strange and silent place? It's too quiet here," he sighed.

A very sultry "Tell me about it!" came from The Telescope on the platform, near the balcony doors, and startled Car-Car out of his melancholy. I don't believe it, he thought, a talking telescope that can hear me!? It was just too much, but then so was The Compact, except we were both automobiles. Could it be that he could actually talk to other species? "Excuse me," asked Car-Car politely, "did you happen to be an automobile at one time?" The Telescope laughed and said, "Surely you jest, darling! I have always been a connection to the stars. It must be time for you to connect with your spirit and leave your material self to itself, or you wouldn't be here." Then she quickly added, before an amazed Car-Car could speak, "And you certainly wouldn't be able to talk with me!"

Car-Car was trying to process this new turn of events. He was beyond trying to talk with The Telescope and waited for her to either speak further or shut up. Either way, Car-Car had had enough surprises for the moment. Apparently The Telescope didn't think so. She went on with her information as though it was a favor she was bestowing on the new piece of furniture in her salon, where she mused on celestial things during the day and ruled the skies at night. Of course she thought of herself as, and acted like, royalty! "You," she drawled as she looked down at Car-Car, "won't be here very long so you'd better not get used to my domain." Car-Car had to smirk at such a remark. "Your domain!?" he repeated. "You can have it! My being here is definitely temporary as is yours. Life is never a one space place as in forever—or hadn't you noticed with your keen sight!?"

The Telescope was intrigued. The strange-looking art knew a thing or two, not like the dunce of a desk who slept without ceasing until any bird visited the balcony. Then the off-key desk would attempt to sing, either with, or back to the bird. It was enough to give The Telescope a nervous breakdown. "You are not a tree with nestlings in your branches," she chided the desk, "You are a hand-carved desk of African descent in North America. Please adjust your focus!" The poor desk would become distracted, the bird would fly away, and sleep would once again wrap its silent arms around the desk that used to be a tree—a tree that had fought a losing battle against becoming something that wasn't a tree firmly rooted in the earth. The desk was stuck in the past and would not let go.

The Telescope concentrated on Car-Car. She scoped that he might know a thing or two—or three even! She cleared her voice and said, "Maybe you are meant to be around for longer than a minute. We will see what we will see. I apologize for being rude." The Telescope waited for the work of art to respond, but Car-Car had had enough for one day. He directed his attention to the sun setting beyond the balcony. As the rosy hues lowered themselves in the sky, a beam of golden light slid between the balcony doors and poured through the rough hole of Car-Car's "hat." Shadow and light played off the sculpture creating new colors and strange, shifting angles. At that moment The Collector came into the room. He was struck anew by how mystical the sculpture appeared in different lights. He was transfixed by its beauty in twilight. It spoke to him in ways that could not be articulated and made him appreciate the purchase even more.

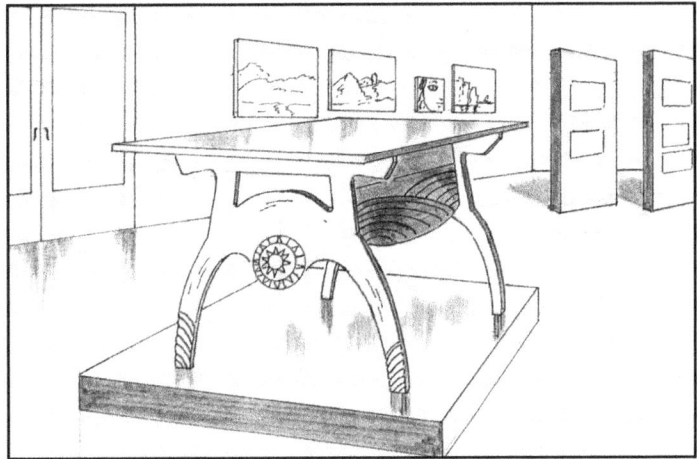

After that The Collector often visited the atrium at eventide to enjoy the daily play of sun on the art that was Car-Car. Many sunsets would find The Collector visiting his new art piece. Then he would join his family for dinner and return when night had come in earnest. That is when, on clear nights, The Collector would open the balcony doors and turn his telescope toward the heavens.

When that first day and night passed in the atrium, Car-Car and The Telescope began to share their thoughts in mutual respect and harmony. Even when The Telescope's first judgment proved to be completely accurate, Car-Car felt the warmth of a second friend and teacher in his life unlike any accidental plot. The main idea The Telescope planted firmly and forever in Car-Car's mind was not to resist when impending and utter change imposed itself on his life. Instead she suggested, Car-Car should seek the spirit within and keep it alive no matter what. The Telescope said that the spirit within is where the soul of the matter lived. She said that even when material is reduced to microscopic dust, the spirit enjoyed enormous breadth and scope and would carry the bearer to heights and spheres of wonder. These thoughts were the ones that Car-Car would keep with him always. They would come back to him many times in the future. Of course Car-Car learned that a telescope was always looking ahead into a future of universal creativity and was used to being quite above most earthly affairs.

Now, just like with The Driver, his rebirth in the junk yard, and a new life with The Artist, Car-Car was growing quite satisfied with his new life in the atrium, though he stayed alert for things to change at any given moment.

The Collector took very good care of his possessions. Professional teams came regularly to dust and polish Car-Car, the desk, and The Telescope.

More years passed and Car-Car could hardly remember having been a car. He felt his usefulness as a work of art as naturally as he had once felt the motor purring in his engine. He felt the presence of the evening sun like an old friend and was not surprised to learn that The Telescope drew upon lessons gleaned from many, many light years out in the deep blue-black depths of sky, but it could not look directly at the sun-star closest to it! It was just another one of the mysteries of life.

Of course Car-Car was as comfortable as he had ever been. Then it happened that his world turned upside-down again! The Collector often brought admirers of art to see Car-Car who had become the art of "Timeless Travel." However, this time something seemed different. Car-Car felt a certain tension in the atmosphere.

There was a woman and a man with The Collector. He felt himself smiling when they gasped in wonder at the beauty of the sunset pouring through the hat-like piece on his top. The golden, purple light cast shadows down and around the glistening sides of red painted steel and chrome. The different shapes and angles thrilled the onlookers. A decision seemed to be

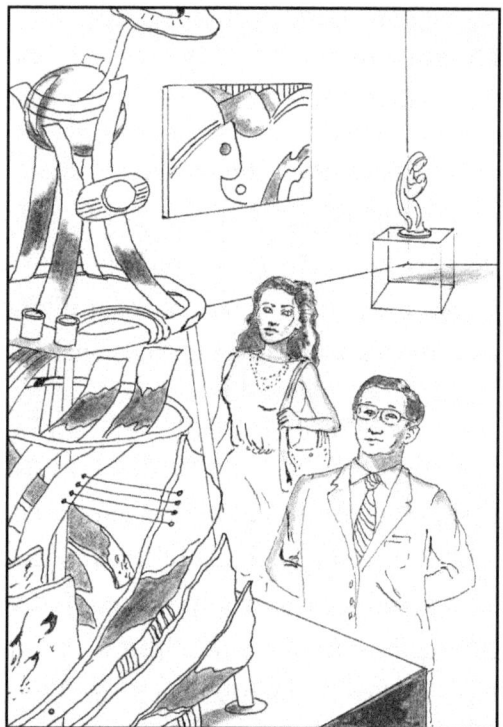

made and a deal was struck in the atrium that very evening. The next thing Car-Car knew he was being carefully crated in a huge wooden box. He was cushioned and surrounded by soft batting and gently placed in a moving van. He was only a bit startled by this turn of events, having learned good lessons about change, but he was sorry he had not been able to say goodbye to his new friend, The Telescope.

Car-Car lost all traces of time while he was housed in the big crate. He had no idea where he was, and he wondered if he were going to stay packed in the crate forever. It was not completely unpleasant, but it was rather lonely. Car-Car had been a lot of things in his life, but he had never been totally alone or lonely. He did not like the trend of these thoughts so he started counting and cherishing his blessings one by one.

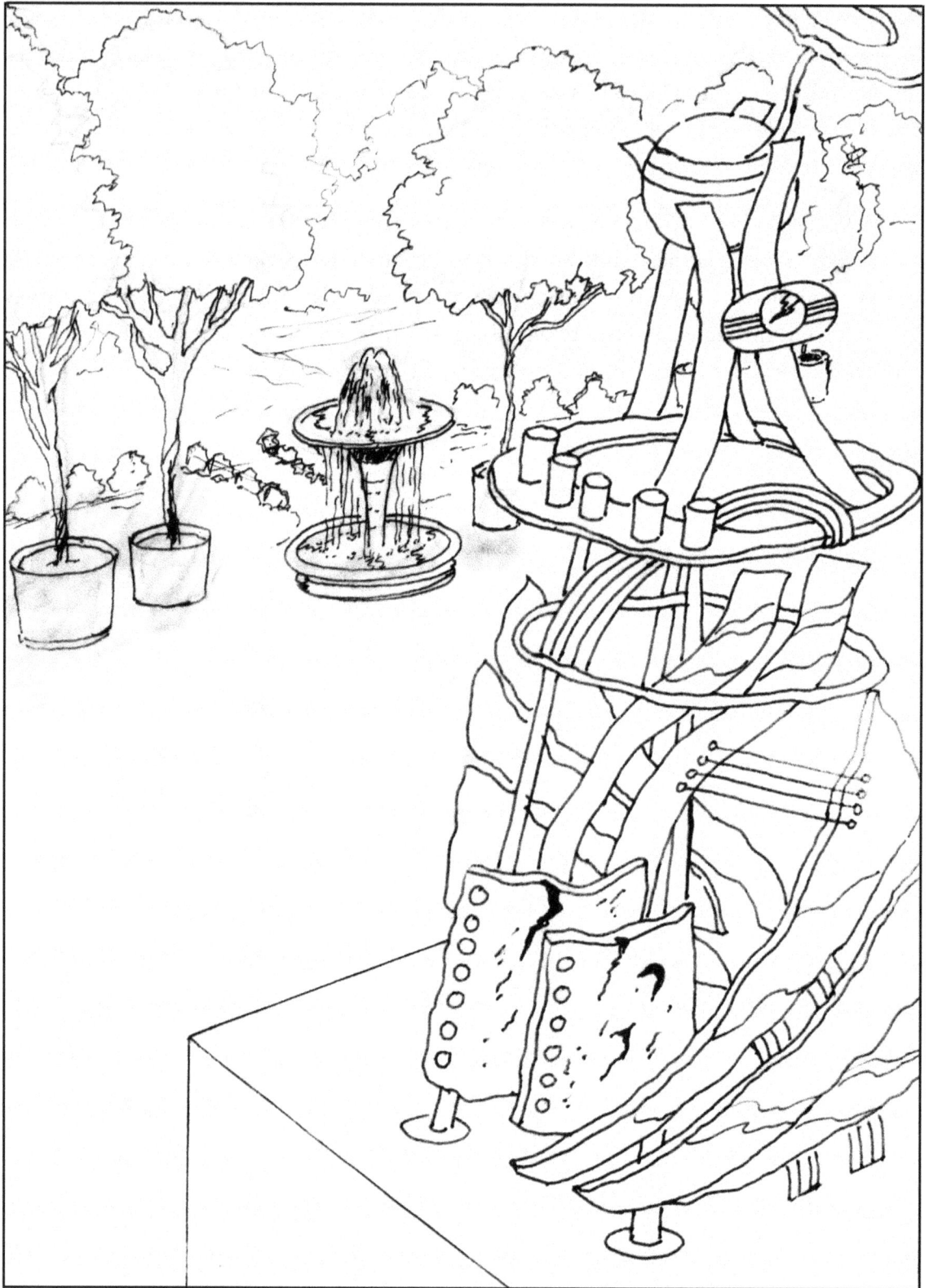

CHAPTER VII

By the time Car-Car had almost run out of blessings to count and appreciate, he heard the creak-creak cracking of the crate being opened. He had been lifted to another space. But that did not surprise him anymore. He had been moved several times since he lived in the crate, but the crate always remained sealed shut after these moves. He felt a new excitement to be getting out of his imposed meditating in the dark. But where in the world was he now?!

With gentle and very careful guidance from The Collector and his associates, Car-Car was placed in a beautiful garden of a great museum. The Collector had amassed so many treasures he began to loan some of them to galleries and museums. Car-Car could not have been happier to be in the outdoors among wonderful trees and flowers. He was placed near two benches and a little waterfall.

The sound of the water was pretty and peaceful. The whole area where he found himself was situated next to a tall black iron fence that connected to a tree-lined street. On that street the traffic of buses, bicycles, people, and oh yes, many cars went by. Why, Car-Car felt right at home. Many people sat on the benches and contemplated the art of Car-Car as they ate their lunches or read their books and papers. Sometimes onlookers sat for long periods of time and did nothing but look and look and look some more. The visitors that came back time and again were the ones lucky enough to have seen "Timeless Travel" during sunset, for Car-Car had been placed in just such a way that—like his place in The Collector's atrium—the setting sun seemed to thread itself through the hole in the top of the sculpture and then spill over the garden in glorious color. The sight not only took the breath away from the museum visitors, but warmed their spirits in a special way. This made Car-Car feel something new: His usefulness had become an instrument of giving people renewed warmth in their spirits and Car-Car was grateful for this unexpected gift. Sometimes only the birds visited the nearby trees or parked themselves on Car-Car's "hat." Sometimes the nights would pass with the stillness only broken by sounds of occasional traffic.

On regular occasions, professional workers came to clean and polish Car-Car which was a good thing since odd turns of weather would leave its marks on the art as well as the benches and the little waterfall. Only the trees took the temperamental weather in stride. When it was time for his cleaning, Car-Car thought it was like having a good massage. It made him feel great and kept him looking as fresh as the day The Artist completed her transformation of him.

One fine afternoon an old man came to sit on the bench nearest Car-Car. He looked at the sculpture a long time and then he leaned over, with a good deal of difficulty, to read the caption inscribed on the plate attached to the pedestal upon which Car-Car rested. "Timeless Travel" read the old man aloud and suddenly Car-Car's senses sprang to a high alertness. He felt like he knew that voice!? Could it truly be? It had to be! Was this old man Car-Car's beloved Driver?! He saw that life and all the years had not only changed Car-Car but had touched and transformed the once athletic-looking man with a full head of hair into a slightly-bent, nearly bald old man who depended on a cane.

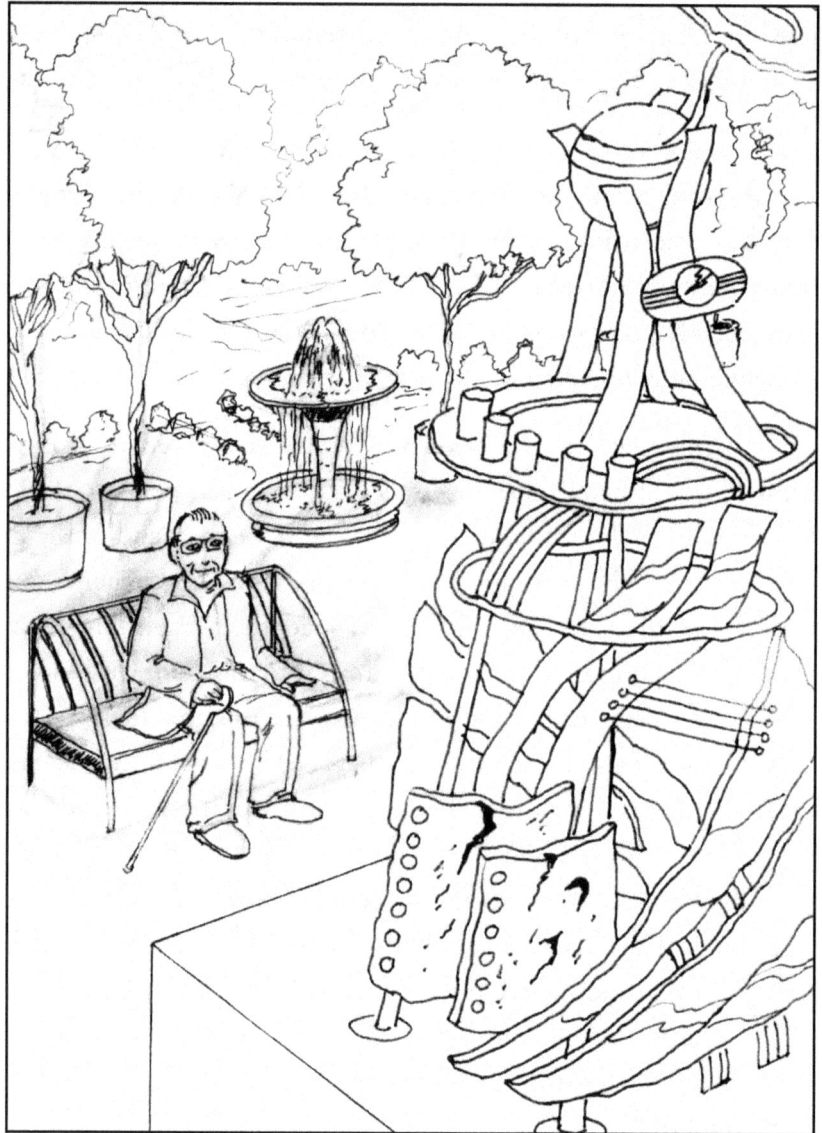

Car-Car felt the whole purpose of his usefulness at once fulfilled yet ready for further employment. Like the sun pouring through the hole in his "hat" it was a most brilliant moment in time!

CHAPTER VIII

The Driver was old now, his son a married man with children of his own. The Driver used his retirement in several ways of leisure and philanthropy. When he saw the new sculpture in the garden of the museum, he was struck by its familiarity. He couldn't put his finger on it, but he knew he would come back to ponder the art piece. And that is what he did almost every day. He sat on the bench and marveled over the shiny red color and the polished chrome that made up the sculpture. The chrome looked a little like part of a distinctive hubcap. "Could it possibly be…?" he wondered. Then he rested his eyes on the battered and incongruous looking, hat-like piece on top of the sculpture. He remembered an auto accident he had been in long, long ago with his favorite car. It must be the color and the dented parts of this art "playing tricks with my mind", thought The Driver. Yet, he couldn't help coming back time and again to sit in awe of the art that took him back to the best years of his life.

As for Car-Car, it was just the usefulness he had been born for. He knew it in the core of his spirit and it made him glow, not from sunlight, but from inner happiness.

THE ONGOING END

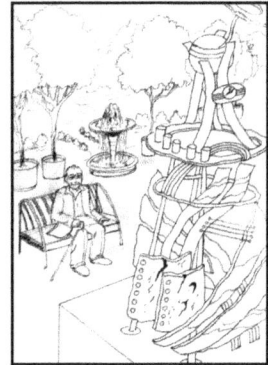

ABOUT THE AUTHOR

Evan was three years old when his mother, Bonita McCall, sat fascinated watching him play with his toy cars. The idea for *Car-Car's Journey* was born at that time.

Three decades later, at the constant urging of her dear friend, Clare, Bonita finally completed writing *Car-Car*! Perhaps that is one of the reasons Bonita refers to herself as a "late-bloomer."

Bonita is a self-professed, life-long "student of love": its constancy, the on-going surrender, the unconditional aspect of the ideal, its healing powers, and the human struggle to let it be. She lives for the evolution of humankind's heart-center to become as important a force as is the world's focus on mind and intellect. She firmly believes this is at the core of Earth's salvation.

Bonita is a world-wide traveler, a poet-writer, and a classically trained pianist. She is a native Chicagoan, but currently resides in North Carolina.

www.ingramcontent.com/pod-product-compliance
Lightning Source LLC
LaVergne TN
LVHW061221060426
835508LV00014B/1393